Exploring Citizenship
Making Choices

Vic Parker

Heinemann
LIBRARY

www.heinemannlibrary.co.uk

Visit our website to find out more information about Heinemann Library books.

To order:

☎ Phone +44 (0) 1865 888066

🖹 Fax +44 (0) 1865 314091

💻 Visit www.heinemannlibrary.co.uk

Edited by Charlotte Guillain and Catherine Veitch
Designed by Ryan Frieson and Betsy Wernert
Picture research by Elizabeth Alexander and Rebecca Sodergren
Production by Duncan Gilbert
Originated by Heinemann Library
Printed in China by South China Printing Company Ltd

ISBN 978 0 431 02534 6
14 13 12 11 10
10 9 8 7 6 5 4 3 2 1

British Library Cataloguing in Publication Data
Parker, Victoria
Making choices. - (Exploring citizenship)
302.1'3
A full catalogue record for this book is available from the British Library.

Acknowledgements

We would like to thank the following for permission to reproduce photographs: Alamy **pp. 4** (© Jupiterimages/Bananastock), **10** (© David Hoffman Photo Library), **11** (© Janine Wiedel Photolibrary/Judy Chapman), **16** (© Varina Patel), **19** (© bildagentur-online/begsteiger), **20** (© Sally & Richard Greenhill), **22** (© Radius Images), **23** (© Roel Meijer), **24** (© Jupiterimages/Bananastock), **26** (© Radius Images); Corbis **pp. 21** (© Matthias Tunger/zefa), **13** (© Gideon Mendel), **27** (© Bryan Allen); Getty Images **pp. 5** (Jamie Grill/Iconica), **6** (Piotr Sikora/Photonica), **8** (Andersen Ross/Blend Images), **15** (Jack Hollingsworth/Photodisc), **12** (Ricky John Molloy/Stone), **29** (Lori Adamski Peek/Stone); Science Photo Library **pp. 18** (Michael Donne), **14** (Ian Hooton); Shutterstock **pp. 7** (© Wouter Tolenaars), **9** (© Mandy Godbehear).

Cover photograph of a girl looking at a salad and a chocolate cake reproduced with permission of Corbis (© Fancy / Veer).

We would like to thank Yael Biederman for her help in the preparation of this book.

Every effort has been made to contact copyright holders of material reproduced in this book. Any omissions will be rectified in subsequent printings if notice is given to the publishers.

All the Internet addresses (URLs) given in this book were valid at the time of going to press. However, due to the dynamic nature of the Internet, some addresses may have changed, or sites may have changed or ceased to exist since publication. While the author and publisher regret any inconvenience this may cause readers, no responsibility for any such changes can be accepted by either the author or the publisher.

Contents

What is citizenship? 4

What are choices? 6

Choosing to think for yourself 8

Choosing to say no 10

Choosing to be friendly 12

Choosing to be fair 14

Choosing what to eat 16

Choosing to spend or save money 18

Choosing entertainment 20

Choosing to be active......................22

Choosing to follow the rules 24

Choosing to tell the truth 26

Making choices and happiness..........28

Glossary 30

Find out more 31

Index..32

Some words are shown in bold, **like this**. You can find out what they mean by looking in the glossary.

What is citizenship?

Citizenship is about being a member of a group such as a family, a school, or a country. A citizen has **rights** and **responsibilities**. Having rights means there are certain ways that people should treat each other.

There are ways to behave when you are out and about.

Being helpful is acting responsibly.

Having responsibilities means you should act or behave in a certain way. The way you behave affects other people. At home and in school you have rights and responsibilities.

What are choices?

Choices are decisions we make about what we want to do. Every day, we all have to make many choices in our lives. Some choices are not so important, such as what colour socks we are going to put on.

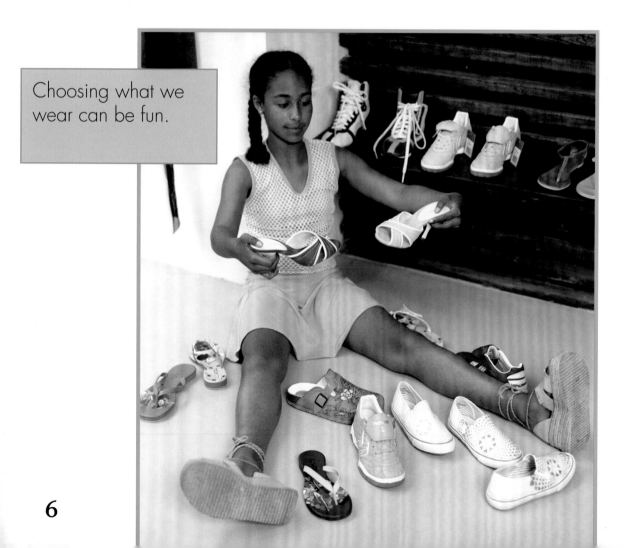

Choosing what we wear can be fun.

Other choices affect our happiness and safety. Our decisions can affect the happiness and safety of other people, too. These choices need a lot of careful thought.

Some choices are very important.

Choosing to think for yourself

Sometimes your friends might have different **opinions** from you. For instance, they might like a different colour or prefer a different game.

Friends can like different things.

You do not always have to choose the same as your friends.

You do not have to agree with your friend.
You do not have to argue with him or her either.
It is fine to choose to disagree and just think
differently. You do not always have to have
the same opinions as your friends.

Choosing to say no

Sometimes you may not feel happy about your friends' choices.

Sometimes your friends might choose to do something unkind or dangerous. You can choose to follow them, or you can choose to say no and do something different. This can be a hard choice to make.

If a friend tries to make you hurt someone else, it is better to walk away.

There may be times when people try to get you to do something that you know is wrong. You might be afraid that if you do not join in, they will be mean to you. If you feel like this, it is best to stop spending time with these people. It is important to have friends who make good choices and help you to make good choices, too.

Choosing to be friendly

Bullying can be saying or doing something that hurts someone else.

Every day, we can choose how we behave towards other people. Being unfriendly to someone again and again can make them feel sad and hurt. This sort of behaviour is called bullying.

When someone is bullying you, you might be afraid to tell anyone. Keeping bullying a secret would probably make you feel very unhappy. If you choose to tell an adult that you **trust**, he or she will help to stop the bullying and help you feel much better.

Sharing your problems is a good choice.

Choosing to be fair

Every day, we have to choose whether or not to be **fair** towards others. For example, do you think it is fair for you to always demand to get your own way? Is it fair if you always choose which television programmes to watch?

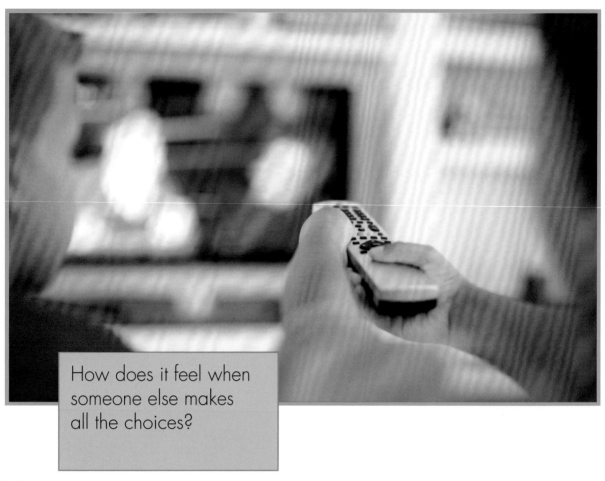

How does it feel when someone else makes all the choices?

Treat others as you would like them to treat you.

If you make a choice that is not fair, you will make other people feel angry or unhappy. Would you like to feel like this? Often, we can make fair choices by thinking about what other people might want.

Choosing what to eat

People have to make choices about what food to eat. Lots of foods are tasty, but some are better than others for giving your body **energy** and helping you stay well. Fruit, vegetables, and wholegrain foods are all healthy choices. Crisps and sweets are less healthy choices.

Choosing healthy foods will make you feel better.

Here are some foods that are not very healthy if you eat lots of them all the time. Next to each one is a healthier food that you could choose instead.

⊘ Unhealthy choice	✔ Healthy choice
Biscuits	Cereal bars
Cakes	Rice cakes
Sweets	Dried fruit
Chips and ketchup	Vegetable sticks and dips
Crisps	Nuts
Ice cream	Frozen yoghurt
Fizzy drink	Fruit smoothie

Think about it

How do you feel if you eat too many sweets or biscuits? Do you feel better when you have eaten more healthy food?

Choosing to spend or save money

When you have pocket money to spend, it is important to make good choices about what you buy. It is better to buy things that last for a longer time, such as comics and toys, than to buy things that last for a short time, such as sweets. Every time you spend money you need to think about these choices.

Sometimes there are so many things to choose from it can be hard to decide.

An adult can help you open a bank account.

You might choose to save your money instead. You could store up small amounts in a money box. For larger amounts, you could choose to keep your money safe in a bank account.

Choosing entertainment

There are many things to do on a computer.

In your free time you might like reading books, watching television programmes and DVDs, or playing computer games. When we choose types of entertainment that are right for our age, they can be great fun.

If we choose entertainment that is meant for adults, we might find it confusing or even scary and upsetting. This is why adults sometimes ask us not to watch or play with certain things. If you are not sure whether something is right for you or not, ask a **trusted** adult to help you choose.

Some books are too easy for us. Others are too hard.

Choosing to be active

Doing gymnastics will make you fit and healthy.

Activities like running, skipping, jumping, dancing, dog-walking, and football make you feel full of **energy** and keep you healthy. Choosing to do one of these activities is a great way to spend your spare time. Think about which activity you would pick as your favourite.

Choosing your favourite exercise will soon make you smile.

If you choose not to do any exercise, you will feel lazy and become unfit. You may become bored and grumpy, too. Doing your favourite activity will soon make you feel much better.

Choosing to follow the rules

Sometimes, people give us **rules** to follow. These rules are usually set for a good reason, such as to keep us safe. For example, at home, you might have rules about things you are not allowed to touch. It is important to choose to follow these rules so you do not get hurt.

Adults set rules because they care about you.

At school, there are also many rules to follow. They are there to make life **fair**, safe, and happy for everyone, so it is a good idea to choose to follow them. Here are some typical school rules. Think about what might happen if you ignored them.

☑ No cheating in tests.

☑ No running in the corridors.

☑ No mobile phones during lessons.

☑ No swinging back on the chairs.

☑ No copying other people's work.

Choosing to tell the truth

Sometimes things go wrong and it is our fault.
It might happen by accident or on purpose.
It is important to choose to tell the truth, even
when it may seem easier to tell a lie or to blame
someone else.

Choosing to tell the truth can be difficult.

Choosing to hide the truth can make you feel miserable.

If you do not tell the truth, you might feel guilty and worried. And if anyone finds out the truth, they may be angry with you. It is always a better choice to tell the truth. Even if an adult is upset about what you have done, they will be pleased with you for being **honest** and for taking **responsibility**.

Making choices and happiness

It is important to make good choices so that you and others can stay happy and safe and so that other people **trust** you.

Good choices include:

- ☑ thinking about other people, not just ourselves
- ☑ choosing to share and take turns
- ☑ choosing to help out at home
- ☑ choosing to try our best with everything
- ☑ choosing to be **honest**
- ☑ choosing to think for ourselves and not be led into things we know are wrong.

Good friends make good choices together.

Making good choices will mean that your life is easier and more enjoyable. You will help yourself and other people to be happy and stay safe.

Glossary

energy power to play and work and do everything you want and need to do

fair way of behaving that treats everyone equally and that everyone is happy with

honest truthful, able to be trusted

opinion point of view, thoughts about something or someone

responsibility something that it is your job to do as a good and helpful member of a group

right how you should be treated by others, in a way that is thought to be good or fair by most people

rule something that says how things should be done, and tells you what you are allowed or not allowed to do

trust know someone is good and honest

Find out more

Books

Citizenship: Being Honest, Cassie Mayer
(Heinemann Library, 2007)

Citizenship: Following Rules, Cassie Mayer
(Heinemann Library, 2007)

Making Good Choices (series) (Picture Window Books, 2004)

Start-Up Citizenship: Making Choices, Louise and Richard
Spilsbury (Evans Brothers, 2007)

Website

www.gogivers.org
This animated site shows children what it means to be part of a
caring society.

Index

activities 22–23

bad choices 10–11
bank accounts 19
books 20, 21
bullying 12–13

choices (what they are)
  6–7
citizenship 4–5
computers 20

energy 16, 22
entertainment 20–21

fairness 14–15, 25
food choices 16–17
friends 8–9, 10, 11, 29

good choices 11, 15, 16,
  17, 18, 22, 28, 29

happiness 7, 28
healthy choices 16, 17, 22
helpful, being 5
honesty 27, 28
hurting someone 11,
  12–13

money, spending and saving
  18–19

no, saying 10

opinions 8, 9

problems, sharing 13

responsibilities 4, 5, 27
rights 4, 5
rules 24–25

safety 7, 24, 25, 28
school rules 25

trust 13, 28
trusted adults 21
truth, telling 26–27